Treasures

A Reading/Language Arts Program

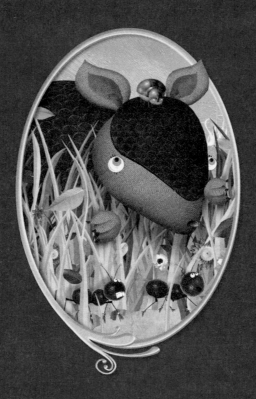

Macmillan/McGraw-Hill

Contributors

Time Magazine, Accelerated Reader

Students with print disabilities may be eligible to obtain an accessible, audio version of the pupil edition of this textbook. Please call Recording for the Blind & Dyslexic at 1-800-221-4792 for complete information.

B

The McGraw-Hill Companies

Macmillan/McGraw-Hill

Published by Macmillan/McGraw-Hill, of McGraw-Hill Education, a division of The McGraw-Hill Companies, Inc., Two Penn Plaza, New York, New York 10121.

Printed in the United States of America

ISBN: 978-0-02-201725-5
MHID: 0-02-201725-9

2 3 4 5 6 7 8 9 DOW 13 12 11 10

Treasures

A Reading/Language Arts Program

Program Authors

Diane August

Donald R. Bear

Janice A. Dole

Jana Echevarria

Douglas Fisher

David Francis

Vicki Gibson

Jan E. Hasbrouck

Scott G. Paris

Timothy Shanahan

Josefina V. Tinajero

Macmillan/McGraw-Hill

The Big Question

Theme Opener 2
Research Activity 4

THEME: We Are Special

Talk About It 6

Nat Can Jump! Words to Know 8

Pam and Sam Fantasy 12
  by Nancy Tafuri

Rules at School Social Studies 26

Writing: **Personal Narrative** 32

THEME: Ready, Set, Move!

Talk About It 34

Jump Over It Words to Know 36

I Can, Too! Rhyming Story 40
  by Cathy Roper, illustrated by Sofia Balzola

Run! Jump! Swim! Science 54

Writing: **Personal Narrative** 60

THEME: Growing Up

Talk About It 62

I Am a Big Kid Words to Know 64

How You Grew Nonfiction 66

Test Practice
Birds Get Big Science 74

Writing: **Narrative (Descriptive)** 76

THEME: Pets

Talk About It 78

Come Down, Flag! Words to Know 80

Flip Fantasy 84
by Ezra R. Tanaka, illustrated by Michael Garland

What Pets Need Science 100

Writing: **Narrative (Descriptive)** 104

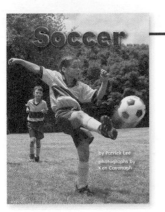

THEME: Playing Together

Talk About It 106

The Gift Words to Know 108

Soccer Nonfiction 112
by Patrick Lee, photographs by Ken Cavanagh

Guess What! Poetry 128
by Michael Strickland

Writing: **Personal Narrative** 130

Show What You Know • REVIEW

Jill and Nat Fiction 132

Cats and Dogs Nonfiction 134

Review Activities 136

Glossary 138

Online Interactive Student Book

Treasures

www.macmillanmh.com

LOG ON ▶ **StudentWorks** *Plus*
Interactive Student Book

VIEW IT 👁

- Preview weekly concepts and selections

READ IT 📖

- Word-by-Word Reading

LEARN IT 🪐

- Comprehension Questions
- Research and Media Activities
- Grammar, Spelling, and Writing Activities

FIND OUT ↖

- Summaries and Glossary in other Languages

LOG ON ▶ **Online Activities**
www.macmillanmh.com

- **Interactive activities** and **animated lessons** for guided instruction and practice

IWB Interactive White Board Ready!

The **Big** Question

What makes you special?

LOG ON ▶ VIEW IT

Theme Video
All About Us
www.macmillanmh.com

What makes you special?

We are all special! The things we like make us special. So do the games we play, the books we read, and the pictures we draw. Our friends, our families, and even our pets all help to make us one-of-a-kind. What makes you special?

Research Activities

Make an "All About Me" book. You can draw your family and friends and your favorite things. You can even include your name and address, your age, and other facts about you.

Keep Track of Ideas

As you read, keep track of all of the things that make you special. Use the **Accordion Foldable** to draw and write on. Think about your favorite games, books, animals, and sports.

FOLDABLES®
Study Organizer

My Name

I can ____   I can ____   I like ____   I like ____   I like ____

Digital Learning

LOG ON ▶ **FIND OUT** www.macmillanmh.com

Interactive Student Book

- **Research Roadmap**
  Follow a step-by-step guide to complete your research project.

Online Resources

- Topic Finder and Other Research Tools
- Videos and Virtual Field Trips
- Photos and Drawings for Presentations
- Related Articles and Web Resources
- Web Site Links

People and Places

Make Way for Ducklings Statues Boston, Massachusetts

Children from all over the world come to see these statues of Mrs. Mallard and her ducklings walking through Boston Public Garden just as they do in Robert McCloskey's beloved book, *Make Way for Ducklings.*

We Are Special

Talk About It

What do you like to do? What makes you special?

Oral Language Activities
We Are Special
www.macmillanmh.com

7

Read To Find Out
How does Nat jump?

Nat Can Jump!

Pat can **jump up.**

Nat can **not** jump up.

Nat can jump up!

Comprehension

Genre
A Fantasy is a made-up story that could not really happen.

Story Structure
Character
Use your Character Chart.

Pam Can	Sam Can

Read to Find Out
What can Pam and Sam do?

Pam and Sam

written and illustrated
by Nancy Tafuri

Award
Winning
Author and
Illustrator

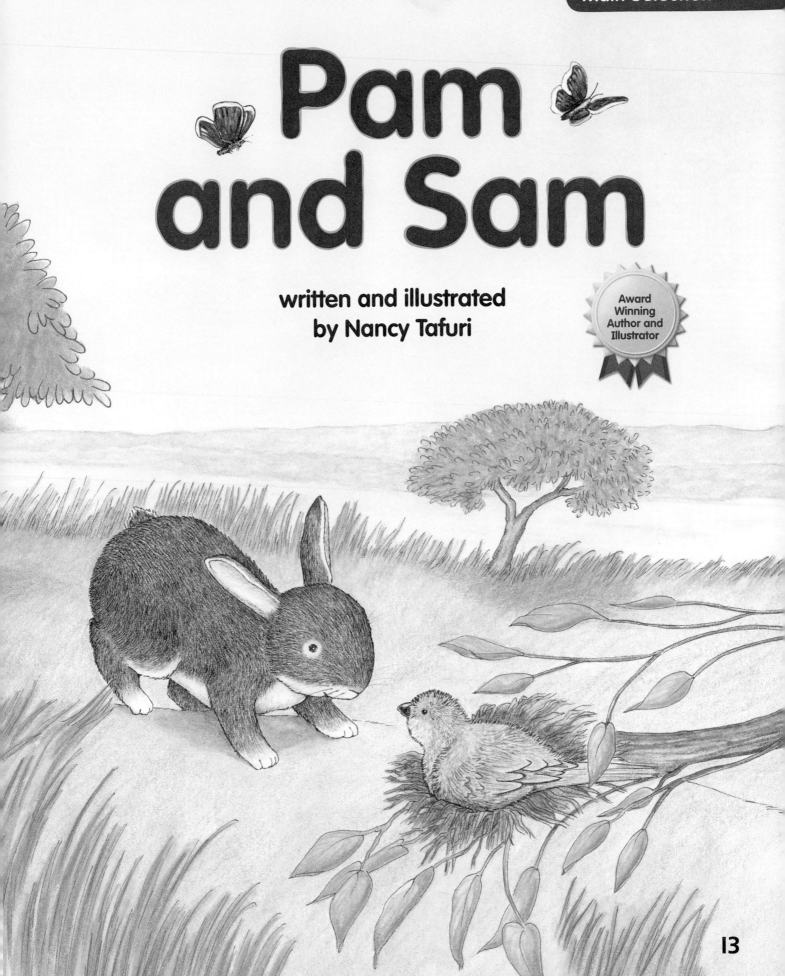

Pam and Sam play.

Pam ran **up**.

Sam ran up.

Pam and Sam ran.

Pam can **jump**.

Sam can **not** jump.

Sam can not go with Pam.

Look at Sam!

Sam can fly!

Pam and Sam can play.

Say Hello to Nancy Tafuri

Nancy Tafuri says, "I live in the country and love telling stories about animals. I especially like to tell stories about good friends like Pam and Sam. I have fun drawing pictures to go with my stories."

Other books by Nancy Tafuri

Author Nancy Tafuri
www.macmillanmh.com

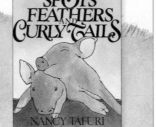

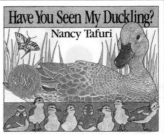

✔ Author's Purpose

Nancy Tafuri wanted to tell a story about friends. Draw a picture of your friend. Write your friend's name.

✔ Comprehension Check

Retell the Story

Use the Retelling Cards
to retell the story in order.

Retelling Cards

Think and Compare

Pam Can	Sam Can

1. Who are the characters
   in this story?

2. What can Pam and Sam do?

3. What can you tell about Pam
   and Sam from the story?

4. How is Nat in "Nat Can
   Jump!" like Sam?

Rules at School

Genre
Nonfiction gives information about a topic.

✔ **Text Feature**
Photographs give more information about the text.

Content Vocabulary
rules
obey
safety

LOG ON ▶ FIND OUT

Social Studies Safety
www.macmillanmh.com

Why do we have **rules** at school?

Rules can help us get along.
Rules can help us stay safe.

We raise our hands.

We listen quietly.

We **obey safety** rules.

We let everyone play!
What are your school rules?

✦ **Connect and Compare**

What rules might Pam and Sam follow to get along and stay safe?

31

Writing

✓ Sentence

A **sentence** tells a complete thought.

Write What You Like to Do

Jen wrote a sentence about painting.

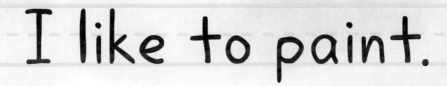

I like to paint.

Your Turn

We can do many things.

What can you do?

Write about something
you like to do.

Grammar and Writing

- Read Jen's sentence.
  Point to the word that tells what Jen
  likes to do.
  Point to the period.

- Check your sentence.
  Does it tell a complete thought?
  Does it end with a period?

- Read your sentence to a partner.

Ready, Set, Move!

How do you like to move? What can you do?

LOG ON ▶ **VIEW IT**

Oral Language Activities
Ready, Set, Move!
www.macmillanmh.com

Jump Over It

Words to Know

over

it

too

———————

can

Read To Find Out

What will the pigs do?

I can jump **over it**.
Can you?

37

I can! I can, **too**.

We can not!

Comprehension

Genre

In a **Rhyming Story**, some words end with the same sound.

Story Structure

✔ **Sequence**

Use your Sequence Chart.

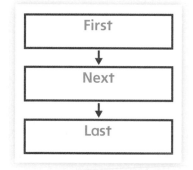

First
↓
Next
↓
Last

Read to Find Out

What will the girl and boy do first, next, and last?

I Can, Too!

by Cathy Roper
illustrated by Sofia Balzola

Can you do what I can do?

I can! I can do **it, too**.

Can you jump **over** a mat?

Can you jump over a hat?

Can you tag a tree?

Can you tag me?

Can you tap, tap, tap?

I can nap, nap, nap.

Can you do what I can do?

I can! I can, too!

Sofia Balzola Can, Too!

When **Sofia Balzola** was a child, she lived in the mountains. Now she lives by the sea in an old house. She loves to illustrate stories about children doing fun things.

Illustrator Sofia Balzola
www.macmillanmh.com

Illustrator's Purpose

Sofia Balzola likes to draw children doing fun things. Draw yourself having fun. Label your picture.

✔ Comprehension Check

Retell the Story

Use the Retelling Cards to retell the story.

Retelling Cards

Think and Compare

1. What does the girl jump over first?

2. What happens after the girl taps the boy? What do the children do last?

3. How would you describe the boy and girl?

4. How is this story like "Jump Over It"?

First
↓
Next
↓
Last

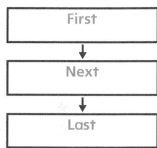

Run! Jump! Swim!

What **helps** animals **move**?

back legs

This kangaroo can jump high.
Strong back legs help it jump.

long legs

This cheetah can run fast.
Long legs help it run.

tail

fins

fins

This shark can swim fast.
Its tail and fins **push** it through
the water.

flipper

flippers

This seal is slow on land.
It is fast in the water.
It swims with wide flippers.

Kids can run, jump, and swim, too.
What helps kids move?

Connect and Compare

Think about *I Can, Too!* How could
animals join the fun?

59

Writing

✔ **Word Order**

The words in a sentence are in an **order** that makes sense.

Write What You Can Do

Tom wrote a sentence about skating.

I can skate.

Your Turn

Look around the room.

Think about something you can do.

Write about it.

Grammar and Writing

- Read Tom's sentence.
  Point to the capital letter at the beginning.
  Point to each word in order.

- Check your sentence.
  Are the words in the correct order?
  Does it begin with a capital letter?

- Read your sentence to a partner.

Talk About It

How have you changed since you were little?

Oral Language Activities
Growing Up
www.macmillanmh.com

Growing Up

I Am a Big Kid

I am a big kid. What can I do?
I can **run**. I can **ride**.

What can I **be**?
I can be me.

How You Grew

How do kids change as they get older?

66

Once you were little.

You learned to talk. You could say "mama" and "puppy."

You could sit.
You could dig.

You could eat at the table.
You could sing a song.

You learned to **run** and **ride**.
You could go fast.

How big are you now?
How big will you **be**?

✔ Comprehension Check

Tell What You Learned

Describe what kids learn to do as they get bigger.

Think and Compare

1. Name one thing kids learn to do when they are little.

2. How do children change as they get older?

3. Why can kids do harder things as they get older?

4. How are the kids in "I Am a Big Kid" different from the kids in "How You Grew"?

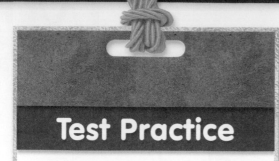

Birds Get Big

First a mother bird lays eggs.

Baby birds grow inside.

Then they hatch.

The mother feeds them.

The babies grow big.

Then they fly away.

DIRECTIONS
Answer the questions.

1 What happens first?

Ⓐ The babies sit on eggs.

Ⓑ The mother lays eggs.

Ⓒ The mother feeds her babies.

2 What happens after the birds hatch?

Ⓐ The birds lay eggs.

Ⓑ The mother feeds them.

Ⓒ The birds make a nest.

3 When the babies are big, they —

Ⓐ sit on eggs

Ⓑ fly away

Ⓒ learn to sing

Write About Kids

First Carly drew a picture.
Then she wrote a sentence.

The writer focused on the topic.

Big kids can ride.

Write to a Prompt

Big kids can do many things.

Write a sentence about what you can do.

Writing Hints

☑ Plan what your sentence will say.

☑ Begin your sentence with a capital letter.

☑ End your sentence with a period.

Pets

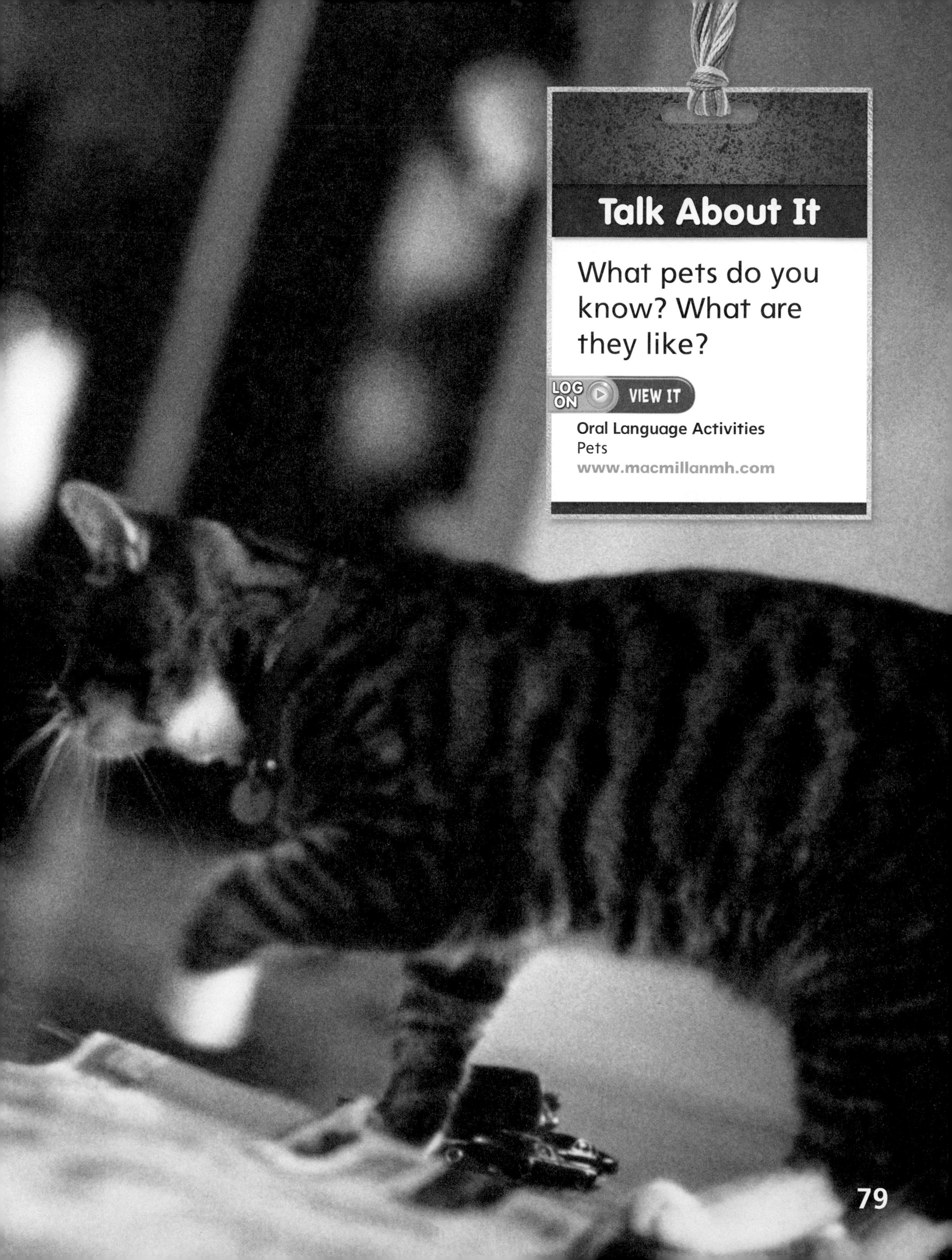

Talk About It

What pets do you know? What are they like?

LOG ON VIEW IT

Oral Language Activities
Pets
www.macmillanmh.com

Words to Know

come
down
good
pull

plan
glad

Read to Find Out
What does Flag
want?

Come Down, Flag!

80

Come down, Flag.
Be a **good** cat!

Flag has a plan.
Flag can **pull** it.

It is for Flag.
Flag is glad!

Comprehension

Genre

A Fantasy is a made-up story that could not really happen.

Story Structure

✓ Plot

Use your Plot Chart.

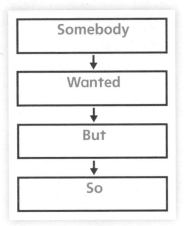

Somebody

↓

Wanted

↓

But

↓

So

Read To Find Out

What will Flip do in school?

FLIP

Award Winning Illustrator

by Ezra R. Tanaka

Illustrated by
Michael Garland

Flip is my pet.
Flip is big.

Flip can not go in.
Flip is sad.

Flip can **pull**!
Flip pulls me in.

Flip and I go to class.

Flip sits.
Be **good**, Flip!

Flip likes class.

The kids like Flip.

Miss Black is mad.
Sit **down**, Flip!

Look at Miss Black!

Flip has a plan.

Flip did it!
The class claps.

Can Flip **come** back?
"Flip can," said Miss Black.
Flip is glad!

Meet Michael Garland

When **Michael Garland** was a child, he loved drawing characters from movies and books. Some of his favorite movies and books had funny creatures in them. So he drew a lot of dinosaurs just like Flip!

Other books by Michael Garland

Illustrator Michael Garland
www.macmillanmh.com

Illustrator's Purpose

Michael Garland likes to draw dinosaurs. Draw a dinosaur. Label your drawing.

✔ Comprehension Check

Retell the Story

Use the Retelling Cards to retell the story.

Retelling Cards

Think and Compare

1. How does Flip feel about not being allowed in school?

2. How does Flip feel about school? How do the kids feel about Flip?

3. What problem does Flip have at school? How does he solve it?

4. How are Flip and Flag in "Come Down, Flag!" alike?

Somebody
↓
Wanted
↓
But
↓
So

What Pets Need

What do pets **need**?

100

Like all **living things**, pets need food.
Some pets eat seeds or plants.

Some pets eat meat or fish.
All pets need fresh water.

Caring for My Rabbit

- Give it food.

- Give it water.

- Change the bedding.

- Brush the fur.

Pets need a safe home.
Pets need our love and **care**.

Connect and Compare

How would you take care of Flip?

Write About a Pet

Writing

✔ **Exclamation**

An **exclamation** is a sentence that shows strong feeling.

Robert wrote about a dog.

Boo is really smart!

Your Turn

Some pets are very special.

Think about a pet you know.

Write to tell why this pet is special.

Grammar and Writing

- Read Robert's writing.
  Which words tell why the dog is special?
  Point to the exclamation mark.

- Check your writing.
  Do you tell why the pet is special?
  Do you use an exclamation mark?

- Read your writing to a partner.

Playing Together

Talk About It

What do you like doing with your friends?

LOG ON ▶ **VIEW IT**

Oral Language Activities
Playing Together
www.macmillanmh.com

The Gift

Rick has a gift.
Ann will **help** him **use** it.

Rick and Ann run **very** fast.

Now the wind lifts it.
It is up, up, up!

Comprehension

Genre
Nonfiction text gives information about a topic.

Text Structure
✔ Author's Purpose
Use your Author's Purpose Chart.

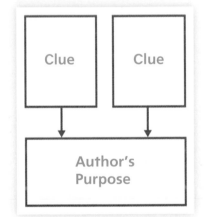

Read to Find Out
Why did the author write *Soccer*?

Soccer

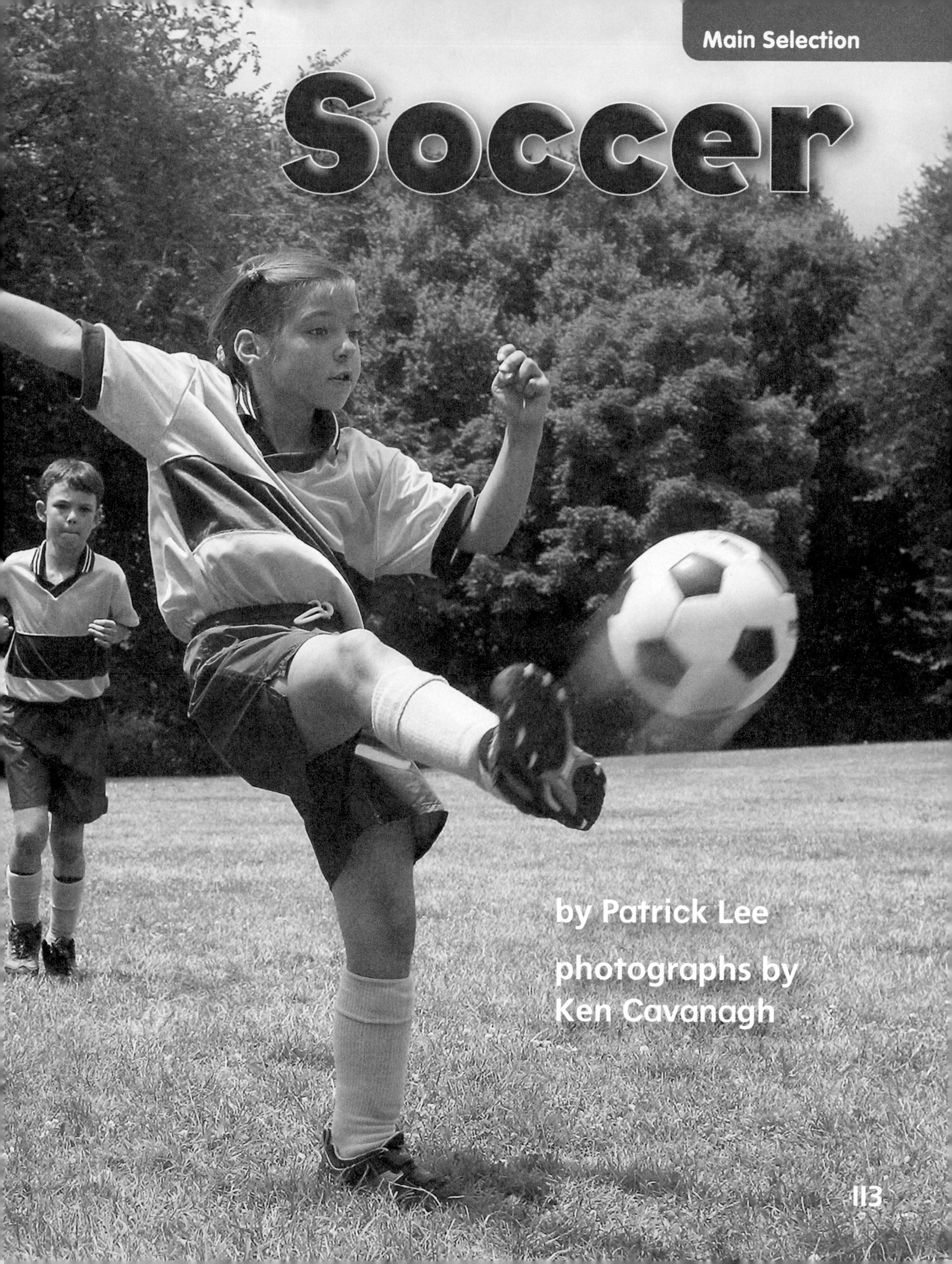

by Patrick Lee

photographs by
Ken Cavanagh

We play soccer.

Hank will **help**.

We run and kick.

I kick and kick.

I am **very** fast.
I am as fast as the wind!

I can not **use** hands.

I can kick the ball.
I will pass it to Jill.

I can zig and zag.
I am very fast.

I can use hands.

Where will the ball land?

I did it.
I am very glad!

Now it is over.
We like soccer!

Meet the Photographer

Ken Cavanagh says, "Many photographers like to take pictures of one or two things, like sports or family events. I enjoy taking pictures of many things. Besides sports, I like to take pictures of people, places, and nature."

 LOG ON ▶ FIND OUT

Photographer Ken Cavanagh
www.macmillanmh.com

Photographer's Purpose

Ken Cavanagh wanted to show how soccer is played. Draw someone playing a sport. Label the picture.

✔ Comprehension Check

Retell the Selection

Use the Retelling Cards to retell the selection in order.

Retelling Cards

Think and Compare

1. Name one thing someone does when they play soccer.

2. How do soccer players move the ball?

3. What is this selection about? What was the author's purpose in writing it?

4. How is the soccer team like Ann and Rick in "The Gift"?

Clue	Clue

Author's Purpose

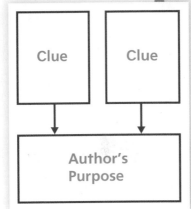

Poetry

Genre
In a **Poem**, words often rhyme.

 **Literary Element**
Words that **rhyme** end with the same sound.

LOG ON ▶ **FIND OUT**

Poetry Rhyming Poems
www.macmillanmh.com

128

READ TOGETHER

Guess What!

by Michael R. Strickland

Black and white
Kicked with might

Smooth and round
Air bound

Passed and rolled
Toward the goal

Rise and fall
A soccer ball.

✔ **Connect and Compare**

- What words in the poem rhyme?
- How is this poem like *Soccer?*

Write About Playing Together

Writing

✔ **Writing Sentences**

A **sentence** begins with a capital letter and ends with a special mark.

Pat wrote about building with blocks.

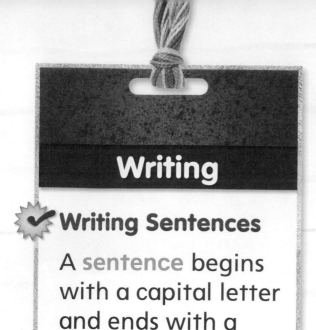

Ray and I play with blocks.

We make big towns!

Your Turn

Think of something you play with your friends. Draw a picture. Write about it.

Grammar and Writing

- Read Pat's **sentences**.
  Point to the capital letter at the beginning.
  Point to the special mark at the end.

- Check your **sentences**.
  Does each begin with a capital letter?
  Does each end with a special mark?

- Read your writing to a partner.

READ TOGETHER

Jill and Nat

Review

Character
Setting
Sequence
Photographs
Labels

Jill is six.

She digs in the sand.

Then she plays with Nat.

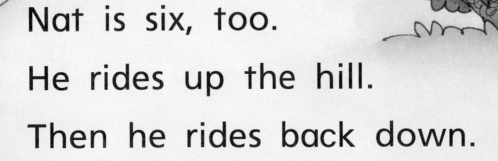

Nat is six, too.

He rides up the hill.

Then he rides back down.

READ TOGETHER

Cats and Dogs

A cat can jump.
A cat can go up a tree.

A cat can move its ears.
It can move its whiskers.
It can lick its paws.

Look at the cat on the grass.
The cat goes, "Purr!"

whiskers

paw

ear

A dog can run.
A dog can jump, too.

A dog has a good nose.
A dog can dig and dig.
It can dig with its paws.

Look at the dog wag its tail.
The dog goes, "Woof!"

nose

tail

paw

135

READ TOGETHER

Word Study

Opposites

- The words tall and short are opposites.

- Work with a partner. Read the words below.

- Name opposites for each.

big	sad
up	fast

Comprehension

What Is Flip Feeling?

- Reread *Flip* on page 84.

- Talk with a partner about what Flip is feeling on each page.

- Talk about why you think he is feeling that way.

Phonics

Make and Read Words

Start with sat.

- Change a to i.
- Change t to p.
- Change s to r.
- What new words did you make?

Writing

Write a Rhyme

- Write a rhyming poem with a partner.
- Think of words that rhyme with cat, box, pig, bag, or man. Think of other rhyming words.
- Use some of the rhyming words in your poem.
- Draw a picture for your poem. Share your poem with the class.

Glossary

What Is a Glossary?

A glossary can help you find the meanings of words. The words are listed in alphabetical order. You can look up a word and read it in a sentence. There is a picture to help you.

fly

fast

138

Sample Entry

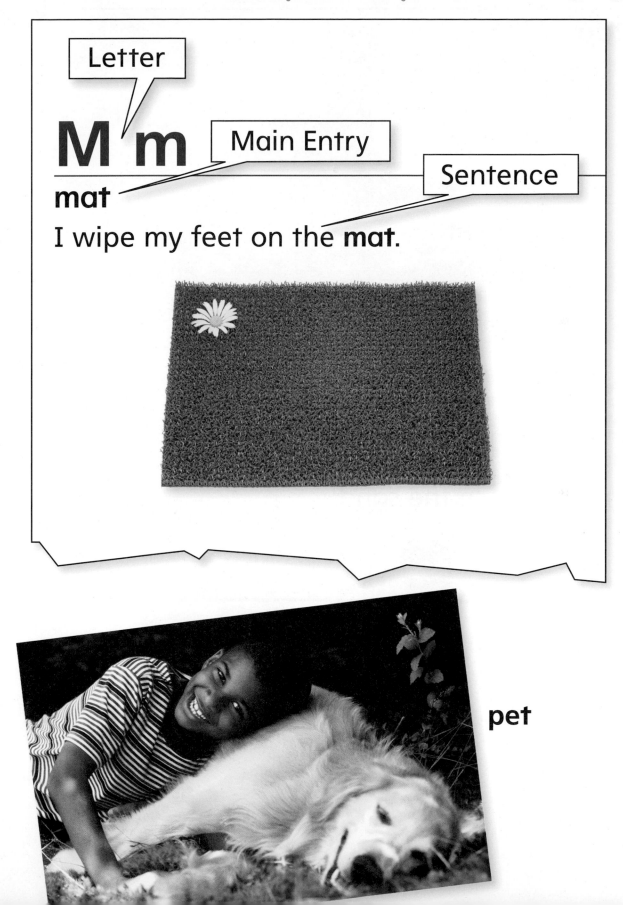

Letter

M m

Main Entry

mat

Sentence

I wipe my feet on the **mat**.

pet

Cc

clap

A seal can **clap**.

Dd

dig

We can **dig** in the sand.

Ff

fast

I run **fast**.

fly

Birds **fly** in the sky.

Hh

hat

The boy has a red **hat**.

help

Amy gets **help** from her dad.

142

Kk

kick

Nan likes to **kick** the ball.

Mm

mat

I wipe my feet on the **mat**.

Nn

nap

Jill takes a **nap**.

Pp

pet

I love my **pet** dog.

144

pull

I **pull** this wagon.

Rr

ride

I go for a **ride** on my bike.

Acknowledgments

The publisher gratefully acknowledges permission to reprint the following copyrighted material:

"Guess What!" by Michael Strickland. Copyright © 2000 by HarperCollins. Reprinted with permission of HarperCollins, NY.

Book Cover, HAVE YOU SEEN MY DUCKLING? by Nancy Tafuri. Copyright © 1996 by Nancy Tafuri. Reprinted by permission of Greenwillow Books.

Book Cover, SPOTS FEATHERS AND CURLY TAILS by Nancy Tafuri. Copyright © 1988 by Nancy Tafuri. Reprinted by permission of Greenwillow Books.

ILLUSTRATIONS

Cover Illustration: Pablo Bernasconi

8–11: Tomislav Zlatic. 12–23: Nancy Tafuri. 26–31: Eileen Hine. 32: Diane Paterson. 36–39: Diane Greenseid. 40–53: Sofia Balzola. 80–83: Steve Haskamp. 84–99: Michael Garland. 108–111: Amanda Haley. 114: Jon Nez. 116: Jon Nez. 118–125: Jon Nez. 128–129: Cheryl Mendenhall. 130: Ken Bowser. 132–133: Benton Mahan. 140, 142-145: Carol Koeller.

PHOTOGRAPHY

All photographs are by Ken Cavanagh or Ken Karp for Macmillan/McGraw Hill (MMH) except as noted below.

iv: Jose Luis Pelaez/Getty Images. v: (tl) Kevin Fitzgerald/Getty Images; (bl) Ken Cavanagh/Macmillan McGraw-Hill. 2–3: Jose Luis Pelaez/Getty Images. 4: Tim Pannell/Corbis. 5: Grant V. Faint/Getty Images. 6–7: Purestock/PunchStock. 24: Courtesy of Nancy Tafuri. 26: Ariel Skelly/Getty Images. 27: Michael Newman/Photo Edit. 28: Airel Skelly/Getty Images. 29: image100/SuperStock. 30: David Young-Wolff/Getty Images. 31: Bluestone Productions/Getty Images. 32: Dynamic Graphics Group/Creatas/Alamy. 33: C Squared Studios/Getty Images. 34–35: Ariel Skelley/Corbis. 52: Courtesy of Ana Costales. 54: Mike Hill/AGE Fotostock. 55: Medford Taylor/National Geographic Image Collection. 56: Tom Brakefield/Corbis. 57: Jeffrey L. Rotman/Corbis. 58: (tc) David Madison/Getty Images; (br) Peter Scoones/Getty Images. 59: Bob Gomel/Corbis. 60: Comstock. 61: (tr) Ingram Publishing/Alamy; (tcr) C Squared Studios/Getty Images. 62–63: Kevin Fitzgerald/Getty Images. 64: David Stoecklein/Corbis; (c) Photodisc/Getty Images. 65: Lawrence Migdale/Photo Researchers. 66: Digital Vision/Punchstock. 67: Photodisc/Punchstock. 68: (t) Blaine Harrington/Corbis; (b) Elyse Lewin/Getty Images. 69: Lawrence Migdale/Photo Researchers. 70: (t) Don Smetzer/Photo Edit; (b) Cheryl Clegg/Index Stock. 71: (tl) Myrleen Ferguson Cate/Photo Edit; (b) David Muscroft/SuperStock. 72: Digital Vision/Punchstock. 74: Darren Bennett/Animals Animals. 76: Brand X Pictures/Getty Images. 77: (cr) C Squared Studios/Getty Images; (b) Bet Noire/Shutterstock. 78–79: Timothy Shonnard/Getty Images. 98: Courtesy of Michael Garland. 100: Gabe Palmer/Corbis. 101: (l) Richard Hutchings/Photo Edit; (r) Robert Maier/Animals Animals. 102: PhotoStockFile/Alamy. 103: Steve Satushek/Getty Images. 104: Kevin Radford/Masterfile. 105: (t) Bildagentur Franz Waldhaeusl/Alamy; (tr) Yiap/AGE Fotostock. 106–107: Blend Images/Jupiter Images. 112–127: Ken Cavanagh/Macmillan McGraw-Hill. 130: Jose Luis Pelaez/Getty Images. 131: Ken Karp/Macmillan McGraw-Hill. 134–135: G.K. & Vikki Hart/Getty Images. 137: (tr) Tracy Montana/PhotoLink/Getty Images; (br) C Squared Studios/Getty Images. 138: Steve Hamblin/Alamy. 138: Norbert Schaefer/Corbis. 139: Stephen Wisbauer /Jupiter Images. 139: Michael Keller/Corbis. 141: Norbert Schaefer/Corbis. 141: Steve Hamblin/Alamy. 142: Digital Vision Direct. 143: Stephen Wisbauer/Jupiter Images. 144: Michael Keller/Corbis. 145: Photodisc Red/Getty Images.